*Sensational*

# SCARVES

# *Sensational*

# SCARVES

## *30 Fabulous Ideas for Twisting, Tying, Draping, and Folding*

Carol Endler Sterbenz

*Principal Photography by*
*Patrick Mulcahy*

SMITHMARK

**A FRIEDMAN GROUP BOOK**

This edition published in 1993 by SMITHMARK Publishers Inc.
16 East 32nd Street, New York, NY 10016

Library of Congress Cataloging-in-Publication Data

Sterbenz, Carol Endler.
 Sensational scarves : 30 fabulous ideas for twisting, tying,
draping, and folding / Carol Endler Sterbenz ; principal photography
by Patrick Mulcahy.
  p.   cm.
 Includes index.
 ISBN 0-8317-7701-X ; $9.98
 1. Scarves.  I. Title.  II. Title : Scarves.
TT667.5.S73  1993                                               93-8402
646′.3--dc20                                                        CIP

*SENSATIONAL SCARVES*
*30 Fabulous Ideas for Twisting, Tying, Draping and Folding*
was prepared and produced by
Michael Friedman Publishing Group, Inc.
15 West 26th Street
New York, NY 10010

Editor: Dana Rosen
Art Director: Jeff Batzli
Designer: Judy Morgan
Photography Director: Christopher C. Bain

Typeset by Classic Type, Inc.
Color separations by Universal Colour Scanning Ltd.
Printed in Hong Kong and bound in China by Leefung-Asco Printers Ltd.

SMITHMARK Books are available for bulk purchase for sales promotion and premium use. For details
write or call the manager of special sales, SMITHMARK Publishers Inc., 16 East 32nd Street,
New York, NY 10016; (212) 532-6600.

All photographs © Patrick Mulcahy, except pages 20, 25, 41, 51 and 52 © Susan Bloch.

# ACKNOWLEDGMENTS

*To Dana Rosen, my editor, and also to the rest of the supportive team at the Michael Friedman Publishing Group: Ann Price, Jenny McMichael, and especially Christopher Bain, for his kind and generous support of each of my books.*

*To Patrick Mulcahy and Susan Bloch, photographers, and the assistants, Rebecca Shavulsky and Neil Bayless, for the beautiful photographs; to the models Corin Casey, Gary Glass, Hope Jackson, Marie Aude, and Gabrielle Sterbenz; and to Genevieve Herr, Jose Garmendia, and Joe J. Simon, hair and makeup.*

*To Lynn Roberts at ЕСНО Design Group for use of the exquisite collection of scarves — again, my deepest appreciation.*

*To Francine Rexer and her daughters, Patricia and Victoria, of Rexer-Parkes of Huntington, N.Y., for the beautiful clothing shown in each of the photographs, and also for the helpful advice and generosity that were beyond my greatest expectations. To David Marsh of Marsh's of Huntington, N.Y., for the fine men's clothing.*

*To Sharon Garland, with love and friendship, for assisting me in styling; and to her daughter, Kristen.*

*Finally, to my daughter Gabrielle, whose sparkle made the project so much fun; and to my husband, John, and my other children, Genevieve and Rodney, who are wonderful. Thank you.*

# CONTENTS

# CONTENTS

*Chapter Three*
# SHOULDERS AND BODICE

Sensational Scarves *is an exciting collection of innovative ways to enhance and extend a wardrobe with the simple addition of one or more scarves. Because scarves come in such a vast variety of sizes, colors, textures, and fibers, they can become indispensable fashion accessories that offer the opportunity to transform the look of an ensemble from mediocre to outstanding.*

*The addition of a scarf to any apparel always adds a splash of color and appealing new texture. By folding, tying, twisting, and draping (and sometimes by combining several of these methods in one design), the entire silhouette of an outfit can be changed. The refined and linear profile of a traditional blazer can be softened and made more romantic with the addition of the sensuous drapes of a paisley wool shawl. A sleek catsuit can be made more dramatic when paired with a bold red hooded cape. A silk scarf detailed with small knots can add delicate accent to the neckline of a plain sweater.*

*But scarves can be more than decorative accessories; they can become apparel itself. It is possible to wrap an oblong wool scarf around the waist for a skirt or kilt, or criss-cross a woven shawl around the head for an exotic turban. The appealing feature of using scarves is that an existing wardrobe can be given a wide range of new style options. Scarves can update last year's fashion, add new interest to favorite staples, and even create whole new looks without large expense.*

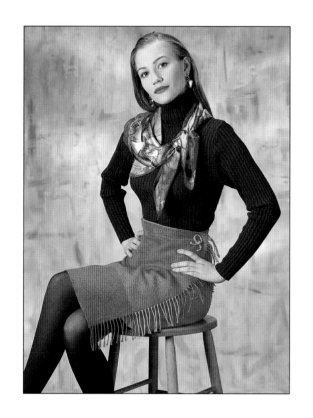

*Whether the scarf is a small pocket square that creates a playful but relatively subtle flourish of color and shape on a classical blazer or a decorated hood and cape that adds dramatic focus, scarves encourage us to express our inventiveness as we adapt them to suit our own personal tastes and style.* Sensational Scarves *provides directions for twisting, tying, draping, and folding thirty innovative designs and traditional favorites that no collection should be without, such as the Windsor headwrap and the chignon. Organized according to where the scarf is worn, this book also progresses thematically from ideas that are suited for casual, daytime wear to those that are more appropriate for formal evening and outdoor wear. The designs range from headbands and head drapes to faux sleeves and wrapped skirts.* Sensational Scarves *also features accessories for men — pocket scarves, an elegant ascot, a sophisticated opera scarf, and more.*

*This collection provides a fashion foundation for your creativity. By following the basic directions, you will be able to create any of the twists, ties, drapes, and folds featured. And as you work with these designs and adapt them to your own fashion needs, you will discover new and exciting ways to wear scarves.* Sensational Scarves *is here to get you started utilizing this wonderful accessory.*

*Chapter One*

HEAD

# WINDSOR-STYLE HEAD WRAP

*The centerpiece of this aristocratic silk scarf, a heraldic crest, is shown to best advantage in this tie. The scarf is the perfect finish to a sweater set in a coordinating color. Although this design is demure and refined as shown, you can create a bolder statement by wearing a scarf in more brilliant colors, such as jewel green, royal blue, and cherry red, and pairing it with a classically tailored blazer or even a big-city leather motorcycle jacket and slim knit skirt.*

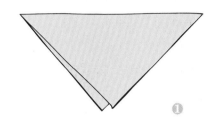

## MATERIALS

1 scarf approximately 30 inches (75cm) square

## DIRECTIONS

① Fold scarf in half diagonally to form a triangle.

② Place folded edge above forehead and tie ends in a double knot under the chin.

# TWISTED AND FOLDED HEADBAND

*The sophisticated elegance of this scarf design is achieved by applying a twisted headband scarf over another scarf folded into a band. Although the scarves pictured here are identical, a pair of scarves in contrasting colors and patterns can be combined to create a bolder look. You may also wish to combine a folded band in velvet with a twisted band in a silk or metallic fabric for a dazzling evening accessory.*

## MATERIALS

2 oblong scarves, each approximately 48 inches (120cm) long and 10 inches (25cm) wide

## DIRECTIONS

*For Folded Headband:*

① Lay scarf horizontally on a flat surface.

② Fold top edge 3 inches (7.5cm) toward center and crease with fingers.

③ Fold lower edge up 3 inches (7.5cm) so that it overlaps upper folded section; crease with fingers.

④ Center scarf on crown of head. Bring ends to back and tie in a double knot.

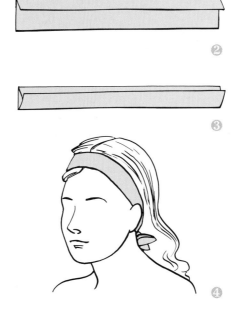

*For Twisted Headband:*

① Holding ends of scarf firmly, twist one end to form a narrow roll.

② Center twisted scarf on folded headband with edges parallel.

③ Bring ends to back of head and tie in a double knot as shown in the photograph.

# BRAIDED HEADBAND

*A simple braiding technique transforms three oblong scarves in brilliant red and gold into an elegant headband with a romantic shoulder drape. Perfect with a turtleneck sweater or billowy poet's blouse, this design is an easy match for leggings, skirts, or jeans.*

## MATERIALS

3 oblong scarves, each approximately 54 inches (135cm) long and 10 inches (25cm) wide

2 lengths narrow silk cord in matching color, each 10 inches (25cm) long

Safety pin

Heavy weight

## DIRECTIONS

① Prepare each scarf following Folded Headband directions, steps 1–3, on page 14.

② Lay the three folded bands on a flat surface with long edges parallel.

③ Place the bands one on top of the other so that the side edges overlap by about ¼ inch (6mm).

④ Secure the bands with a safety pin about 12 inches (30.5cm) from the top edges.

⑤ Place a heavy weight on top section to hold it in place during braiding.

⑥ Braid the three bands together to within 12 inches (30.5cm) of bottom ends.

⑦ Secure braid at bottom using silk cord.

⑧ Remove weight and safety pin, and secure braid at top using silk cord.

⑨ Center braided headband on crown of head. Bring ends to back and tie in a double knot; allow ends to drape softly over shoulders.

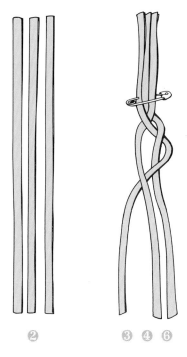

② ③ ④ ⑥

⑦ ⑧

# CHIGNON

*Reminiscent of the sixties but truly a timeless wrap for hair pulled back in a bun, the chignon remains a classic look for any occasion. Perfect when paired with a creamy silk blouse or raincoat, the chignon adds effortless polish to any outfit.*

*For daytime, choose scarves in paisley, stripe, or plaid patterns that harmonize with blazers, twisted cable sweaters, or suede cropped jackets. For evening, choose scarves that are gauzy and sheer or ones that have metallic thread for extra sparkle. Wrap a length of silk roping around the chignon for an even dressier trim.*

①

②

## MATERIALS

1 scarf approximately 20 inches (50cm) square

(Note: Use the chignon tie to cover a hairbun at the back of the head.)

## DIRECTIONS

① Fold scarf in half diagonally to form a triangle.

② Place center of folded edge above bun. Draw scarf around bun, crossing ends behind drape.

③ Bring ends up to top of bun and cross again.

④ Bring ends down in front of drape and tie in a double knot.

⑤ Bring loose drape of scarf up and tuck behind knot to finish.

*Since the silk scarf tends to slip if not anchored with bobby pins, have a few on hand when first draping the scarf over the bun.*

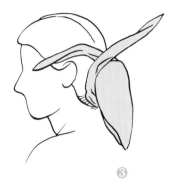

③

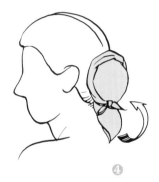

④

⑤

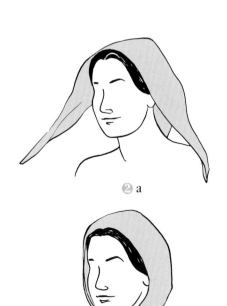

② a

# *C*LASSIC HEAD WRAP

*Nostalgic yet always modern, this particular head wrap has been associated with such luminaries as Greta Garbo, Marlene Dietrich, and Jacqueline Kennedy Onassis. A true classic, this versatile and simple style can change the mood of any outfit, as it looks terrific in virtually any weight fabric and/or pattern. It is important, though, to use a large square scarf that can be folded diagonally and whose ends are long enough to easily cross from underneath the chin to the back of the neck, where they are tied in a double knot.*

*You might want to try pairing a gauze scarf with a sheer blouse for a dressy look. For something more casual, coordinate a large polka-dot scarf with a crisp cotton blouse, a flared skirt, and cat's-eye sunglasses. To achieve both warmth and style in cooler weather, tie on a plaid wool scarf and tuck it into the collar of a short swing coat.*

② b

## MATERIALS

1 animal-print scarf approximately 30 inches (75cm) square

## DIRECTIONS

① Lay scarf on a flat surface with points at top and bottom. Fold top point down 2 inches (1.25cm) past center.

② Place scarf over head (a) and cross ends under chin (b).

③ Bring ends around to back of neck and tie in a double knot.

④ Tuck loose drape of scarf over knot to finish.

①

③

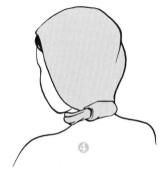

④

# FULL TURBAN

*The natural fabric of this lightweight, woven scarf is dyed in bright magenta, navy, and turquoise. Oversized and fringed, the scarf is wrapped in a turban style very much like you would wrap a bath towel around your hair after a shower. Because the method of wrapping the scarf is so easy, you'll consider the turban the perfect accessory for those times when a dramatic and elegant cover-up is called for.*

*As an alternative, you can pair a banana-yellow scarf, refined in contour but having a drama all its own, with a cotton shell in a matching color and pile on beaded bangles and oversized hoop earrings. For something more understated, wrap a matte satin scarf in creamy ivory in a full turban and pair it with a shiny satin blouse in a matching color.*

## MATERIALS

1 oblong woven cotton scarf approximately 78 inches (195cm) long and 24 inches (60cm) wide

Small self-adhesive Velcro dots

## DIRECTIONS

① Position center of scarf at back of neck. Holding ends taut, wrap scarf around sides of head toward top.

② Tie a knot at crown of head.

③ Wrap free ends around head, crossing at back of neck.

④ Continue last wrap up over top of head and tuck into headband at front.

⑤ Adjust knot and spread fabric to cover head completely.

⑥ Attach Velcro dots to secure overlaps, if necessary.

*Scarves that have texture are most suited for this wrap since shiny fabrics like silk and satin tend to slip.*

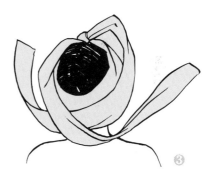

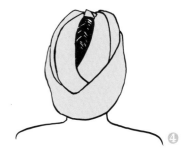

# HALF TURBAN

*Popular in the 1940s, the half turban takes on a contemporary look when made of a metallic stretch knit scarf tied in a classic topknot. The knit fabric allows the wrap to fit snugly and comfortably without slippage, while the metallic thread adds sparkle and elegance. Worn with or without a matching dickie and a sleek black jacket, this turban is the perfect way to dress up an outfit in an instant.*

*Stretch knits work best with this style, but silks and synthetics are good choices, too; with these fabrics, however, the topknot should be positioned closer to the forehead to minimize slippage and several bobby pins should be used to secure the scarf to the back of the head. Solid colors and overall designs are the most flattering patterns to use. Bold colors and textured fabrics will add the most visual interest.*

---

## MATERIALS

1 stretch knit scarf with metallic thread approximately 40 inches (100cm) long and 10 inches (25cm) wide

## DIRECTIONS

① Holding ends of scarf firmly, place center of scarf at middle of back of neck, bringing remaining fabric to top of head.

② Tie a knot at crown of head.

③ Tie a second knot.

④ Tuck ends of scarf under headbands formed by tying knots in steps 2 and 3.

⑤ Adjust knots and headbands by spreading fabric to create turban look.

*Chapter Two*

# NECK

# EVENING SHAWL

*This drape is serene and sublime, a beautiful accessory to dress up a simple silk jacket or dress, or to encircle the collar of a dressy coat. Incredibly easy to wrap, the shawl will always give the look of luxury and romance. For daytime, choose a scarf in soft wool or cashmere to match a roomy sweater or blazer. Combine the palest of colors together—pale yellow with pale teal, cream with dusty rose—or for a bolder look, coordinate richer colors like hunter green and rust, or maroon and navy.*

## MATERIALS

1 oblong silk scarf approximately 68 inches (170cm) long and 22 inches (55cm) wide

## DIRECTIONS

① Hold the scarf at one short end, allowing the full length to hang down.

② Place the end over the right shoulder so that it has a back drape of approximately 8 inches (20cm).

③ Carry the excess across the front of the neck to the left shoulder and bring it up and around the head; the drape will fall down the right front of the body.

④ Carry the excess drape across the chest below the neck and pass it over the left shoulder to the back.

⑤ Adjust the folds as desired.

# DECORATED CAPE AND HOOD

*A cape and an oblong scarf, perfect pieces to wear as separates or together, create this smashingly romantic hooded cape. The oblong scarf is folded and sewn along one side to create the hood, then accented with braided trim; the ready-to-wear cape in matching color is decorated with matching trim along the front panels. The flow and drape of this ensemble make it the perfect evening cover, especially when worn over a black velvet catsuit or floor-length gown in black wool crepe.*

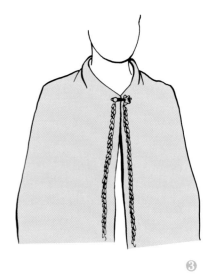

③

## MATERIALS

### For Decorated Cape:

1 red wool cape

2 yards black braided trim

1 red or black frog fastener

Thread to match

Hand-sewing needle; pins

Sewing machine

### For Hood Drape:

1 red oblong wool scarf approximately 60 inches (150cm) long and 16 inches (40.5cm) wide

1³/₄ yards (1.5m) black braided trim

Thread to match

Hand-sewing needle; pins

Sewing machine

## DIRECTIONS

### For Decorated Cape:

① Pin trim along outside edges of front cape opening; baste, then remove pins.

② Machine-stitch in place; remove basting.

③ Place cape over shoulders and position frog on outside for neck closure. Mark, pin, and hand-sew frog halves to sides of cape; remove pins when done.

### For Hood Drape:

① Pin braided trim to one long edge of scarf; baste, then remove pins.

② Machine-stitch in place; remove basting.

③ Fold scarf in half widthwise, with braided edge on outside.

④ Beginning at fold, sew a ³/₈-inch (9mm) seam along the untrimmed edge for 14 inches (35.5cm) to form hood.

⑤ Clip corner and turn to right side.

⑥ Place hood on head, centering over crown.

⑦ Cross ends in front of neck and drape over shoulders to back.

⑧ Adjust width of hood by folding back edge to frame face and reveal braided trim.

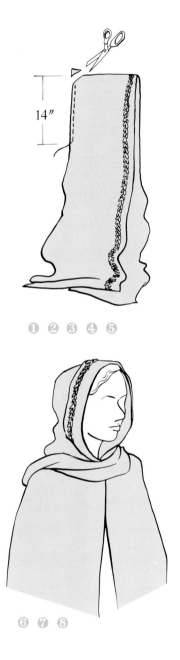

14"

① ② ③ ④ ⑤

⑥ ⑦ ⑧

# TWISTED JACKET COLLAR

*The soft twists of this ordinary wool scarf form a double-tiered collar on this cropped jacket, enhancing the brilliant indigo color of its houndstooth weave. Equally suitable for use on a crew-neck or jewel-neck sweater, the twisted scarf is gently wound around the neck and tucked slightly under the edge of the neckline. Instead of picking up one of the colors in a multicolored fabric, try choosing a scarf in the same color as a monochromatic jacket. Or, coordinate the scarf with the color of a skirt or a pair of trousers. The look of the twisted collar is quite sophisticated, and the feel of the scarf around the neck is always luxuriously cozy.*

## MATERIALS

1 oblong wool scarf in color matching chosen jacket, approximately 60 inches (150cm) long and 15 inches (37.5cm) wide

## DIRECTIONS

❶ Center scarf at back of neck; bring ends to front.

❷ Twist left end gently, then bring across front of neck and around to back.

❸ Twist right end and place across neck directly below first twist to form collar.

❹ Tuck loose ends under collar at back.

❺ Adjust twists at front and tucks at back to conceal edge of jacket neck.

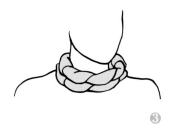

# BOW TIE

*The luxury and softness of silk is evident in this sophisticated combination. The two-pocket shirt and the full bow tie blend in alluringly gentle contours and create a very flattering ensemble for daytime or evening wear. The ruby-red scarf was chosen for its beauty as well as the contrast it created against the cream-colored blouse. For a less dramatic combination, try pairing a scarf and blouse in shades of dove gray or white, or for another strong statement, coordinate a navy blouse with a burgundy scarf in a paisley design.*

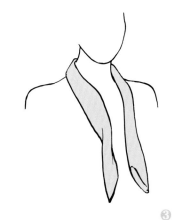

## MATERIALS

1 scarf approximately 48 inches (120cm) long and 10 inches (25cm) wide

## DIRECTIONS

① Lay scarf on a flat surface. Fold one-third toward center along long edge from top to bottom.

② Fold one-third again from bottom to top to form folded band.

③ Center folded band at back of neck; bring ends to front.

④ Cross ends at front of neck and tie in a bow.

⑤ Adjust loops and ends as desired.

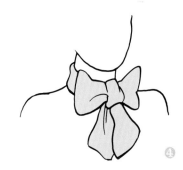

# BUSTLE-STYLE COLLAR WITH RING

*A new option for dressing up the classic white shirt, a fringed scarf is looped through a pretty gold ring and pulled into a bustle shape at the neckline. Consider using an accordion-pleated scarf in ivory with a silk blouse for a more vintage look, or a textured wool scarf with a tailored wool shirt for something more informal.*

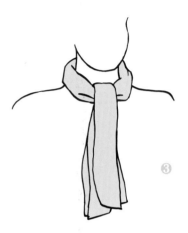

## MATERIALS

1 oblong scarf approximately 54 inches (135cm) long and 10 inches (25cm) wide

1 ring approximately ³/4 inch (2cm) in diameter

## DIRECTIONS

① Fold scarf in half lengthwise.

② Center scarf at back of neck with fold at top; bring ends to front and tie in a single knot.

③ Overlap ends to conceal knot.

④ Insert ends of scarf through ring held 5 inches (12.5cm) below knot.

⑤ As you pull scarf through, slide the ring up to neck so scarf forms loop.

⑥ Adjust folds of loop to full width to form bustle, allowing loose ends to cascade below.

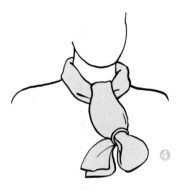

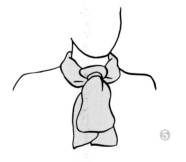

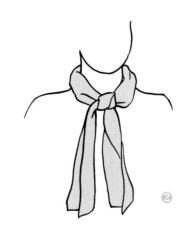

# KNOTTED NECKLACE

*The simplest of ties, the knotted "necklace" looks particularly pretty and demure worn with this cabled sweater in dusty pink. The idea behind this tie is to create a sculptured detail that brings the eye to the neckline or the collarbone. The scarf is first folded into a band, and then knots are carefully tied and flattened along the length of the band. The look shown here is very feminine and sweet, but this design rendered in a metallic scarf would make a dazzling evening accessory.*

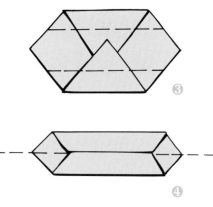

## MATERIALS

1 scarf approximately 30 inches (75cm) square

## DIRECTIONS

*For Folded Band:*

❶ Lay scarf on flat surface with points at top and bottom.

❷ Fold top point down 2 inches (5cm) past center.

❸ Fold bottom point up 2 inches past center, so points overlap.

❹ Fold top edge down to horizontal center. Fold bottom edge up to meet it.

❺ Fold in half lengthwise along horizontal center to form folded band.

❻ Tie folded band as shown in following directions.

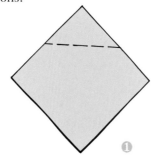

*For Tie:*

❶ Place folded band on flat surface.

❷ Cross A over B to form a small loop at center of band.

❸ Bend A down and insert through loop; pull both ends of scarf gently to form smooth, flat knot.

❹ Form a second loop about 1 inch (2.5cm) to the left of center knot. Insert free end of band through loop to form second knot.

❺ Repeat step 4 to make a third knot 1 inch (2.5cm) to the right of center knot.

❻ Holding knotted necklace at both ends, bring up around neck so knots are centered in front.

❼ Bring ends to back of neck and tie in a double knot.

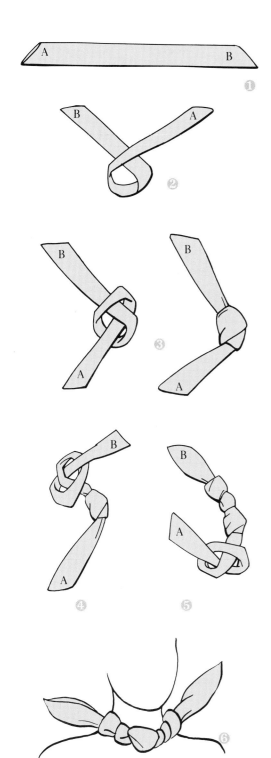

# MODIFIED ASCOT

*The modified ascot is a very aristocratic look, particularly when tied in an elegant silk fabric that drapes easily about the neck. The modified ascot is also less formal than the traditional ascot, for the small front knots add a softer, more feminine touch. This ascot is extremely versatile and will complement far more than the standard blazer. Try pairing this scarf with a V-neck sweater or dress, or a suede, varsity-style jacket. The best scarf patterns for this look are small, overall designs, geometrics, and stripes.*

## MATERIALS

1 silk scarf approximately 30 inches (75cm) square

## DIRECTIONS

① Fold scarf in half diagonally to form a triangle.

② Place center of scarf at front of neck.

③ Bring ends to back of neck and cross.

④ Bring ends to front again and tie two loose knots, centering them below chin.

⑤ Arrange drape as desired.

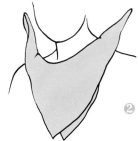

# NECK DRAPE* AND WRAP SKIRT

*The soft drape of floral silk is perfect with this long-sleeve turtleneck, especially as it echoes the melon palette of the slim wrap skirt in cashmere-soft plaid wool. An elasticized waist at the back of the skirt creates a flattering contour, and the front fringe adds fresh appeal.*

## MATERIALS FOR NECK DRAPE

1 print scarf approximately 33 inches (82.5cm) square

*Design by Sharon Garland

## DIRECTIONS

① Lay scarf on a flat surface with points at top and bottom.

② Fold top point down 2 inches (5cm) past center.

③ Place scarf on shoulders, centering bottom point at middle of back.

④ Bring ends to front and tie in a loose double knot at center of neck.

⑤ Slide knot to left collarbone, adjusting drape as desired.

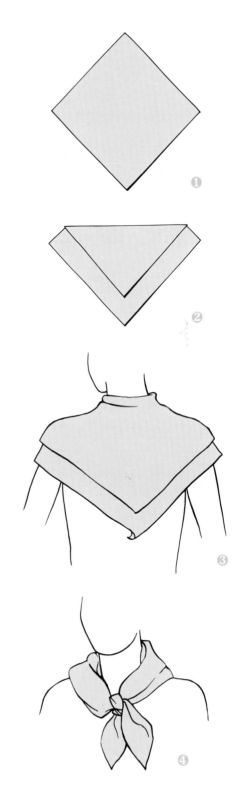

# MATERIALS FOR WRAP SKIRT

1 oblong wool scarf with fringed ends, approximately 60 inches (150cm) long and 22 inches (55cm) wide

10 inches (25cm) elastic, 1 inch (2.5cm) wide

Hand-sewing needle; pins

Thread to match

Shoelace 30 inches (75cm) or longer

2 hooks and eyes

Decorative pin

# DIRECTIONS

① Lay scarf horizontally on a flat surface, wrong side up.

② Fold top long edge down 1½ inches (4cm); press with an iron set to "steam" to form waistband.

③ Unfold waistband. Center elastic on scarf directly below foldline. Pin in place.

④ Sew one end of the elastic to the scarf; remove pins.

⑤ Sew a shoelace to the opposite end of the elastic and position it so that it extends beyond the fringe of the scarf.

⑥ Fold waistband down and pin along long edge; baste, then remove pins.

⑦ Sew a seam 1¼ inches (3cm) from folded edge to form waistband casing.

⑧ Pull shoelace to stretch the elastic, gathering back of waistband until desired reduction in measurement is achieved. Pin end of elastic through waistband and top-stitch to secure. Gently remove shoelace by pulling it through casing as far as it will go; then snip with scissors.

⑨ Center elastic portion of waistband at back of waist (a). Bring left end of scarf across front to right hip (b); bring right end across front to left hip. Adjust overlap until comfortable; mark position for hooks and eyes on waistband.

⑩ Sew hooks to inside edge of waistband, eyes to outside edge.

⑪ Center scarf on back of waist. Bring left end around to front and across to right hip. Bring right end around to front and across to left hip. Connect hooks to eyes and add decorative pin as desired.

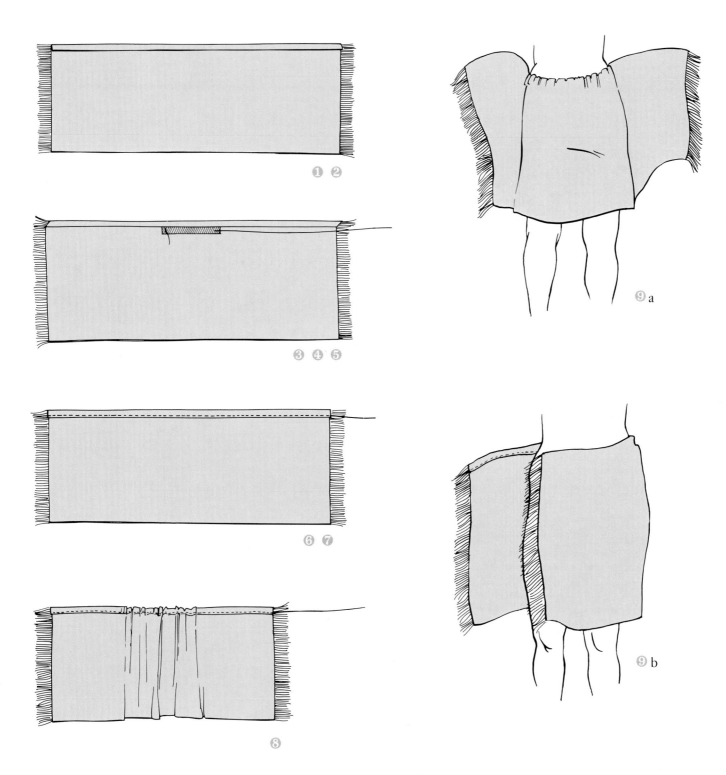

①②

③④⑤

⑥⑦

⑧

⑨a

⑨b

*Chapter Three*

# SHOULDERS
# AND BODICE

# SINGLE-SHOULDER DRAPE

*Artfully draped, this chenille scarf in hunter green, burgundy, and gold accentuates the classic lines of the cropped jacket. Gathered in soft, even folds at the shoulder, the length of fabric drapes in a soft curve across the bodice of the jacket and is secured above the right hip with a decorative pin. For a variation on this design, allow the long fringed end of the scarf to cascade down, breaking the line of the jacket and introducing a splash of color to a skirt or trousers in a coordinating color.*

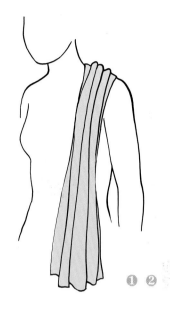

## MATERIALS

1 oblong plaid wool scarf approximately 68 inches (170cm) long and 12 inches (30.5cm) wide

Decorative pin

## DIRECTIONS

❶ Center scarf on left shoulder, allowing ends to drape softly to front and back.

❷ Adjust width of scarf by gathering soft even folds at shoulder until desired look is achieved.

❸ Drape front end across lower bodice, ending above right hip. Secure folds with a decorative pin.

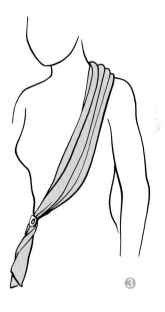

# SHOULDER DRAPE

*The understated elegance of this drape belies the simplicity of its arrangement. Placed off-center and tied on the shoulder, the scarf's sensuous folds soften the straight lines of a dress and add a charming contrast.*

*Small Velcro dots are an easy way to keep this wrap firmly in place; just strategically position the dots on the underside of the scarf and on top of the garment, and press them together. Using Velcro dots also enables you to use smoother, lighter fabrics, such as rayon, silk, and satin, as these tend to slide about if they are not held down in some way.*

## MATERIALS

1 floral-patterned silk scarf approximately 30 inches (75cm) square

Small self-adhesive Velcro dots

Decorative pin

## DIRECTIONS

① Fold scarf in half diagonally to form a triangle.

② Place scarf on shoulders, centering bottom point on left shoulder.

③ Tie ends into a loose double knot on right shoulder.

④ Arrange folds of scarf; use Velcro dots to firmly position drape, if necessary.

⑤ Add decorative pin.

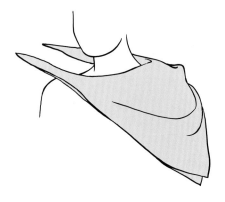

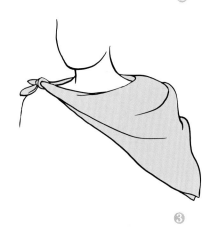

# SHOULDER WRAP

*This pretty wrap made from a floral scarf highlights the neckline and enfolds the shoulders, and is also beautiful when worn with a strapless dress. When fringe, tassels, or beadwork is added to the selvages, the wrap is an ideal complement to evening wear. For a less formal look, try pairing a white cotton strapless top with a shoulder wrap in a compatible cotton. The best scarves for this style are those that tend to stay in place, so choose fabrics that are rougher rather than smoother in texture. This design can be easily adapted for any season simply by using scarves of different weights and colors.*

## MATERIALS

1 floral-patterned scarf approximately 40 inches (100cm) square

## DIRECTIONS

① Fold scarf in half diagonally to form a triangle.

② Centering scarf on back, bring ends forward and place scarf just off the shoulders.

③ Tie ends into a double knot at center of chest.

④ Adjust folds of scarf as necessary.

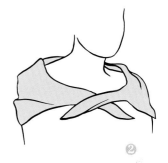

③ Adjust scarf over left shoulder, allowing the full length to drape down the arm for a faux sleeve. Pin the scarf from the inside to keep it in place, if desired.

# SHOULDER DRAPE WITH FAUX SLEEVE

*A diaphanous drape of sheer silk creates this alluring and elegant faux sleeve. Don't be afraid to experiment with all kinds of variations on the basic tie, where the scarf cascades freely along your arm. Instead, after tying the scarf around your neck, secure the bottom drape by tying the ends around your wrist. Or, if you prefer, drape the scarf off the shoulder so that it billows out as you walk, as shown in the smaller photograph. You can also sew beads to one edge of the scarf to create the look of a bracelet, or add a delicate crocheted edge for a faux cuff.*

*The appeal of this drape is that it adds romance to the most basic of dresses, thereby transforming an ordinary dress into one that is unique and extraordinary. But don't limit its use to strapless or sleeveless dresses only; try it with a lace bodysuit too. This design works best with sheer scarves because they act like a veil and allow the arm to show through in a stately but sensuous way.*

## MATERIALS

1 scarf approximately 30 inches (75cm) square

## DIRECTIONS

① Hold scarf at top corners and place around neck at front. Bring ends to back and tie in a double knot.

② Slide knot to right shoulder.

# DOUBLE-BODICE STOLE

*A dramatic off-the-shoulder stole made from two sheer scarves secured at each shoulder adds elegance to this black fitted evening dress. Once you have created the basic stole, you can wear the design in several other ways. Allow one rosette to rest on the back of the neck and the other rosette to rest below the left shoulder, with the ends of the scarves cascading to the left wrist, as shown in the smaller photograph. Alternatively, place one rosette at the center of the dress bodice and the second rosette at the center of the back bodice so that the scarves resemble "straps" that go over the shoulders. This scarf design is so versatile, you will want to experiment in creating your own new and exciting variations.*

## MATERIALS

2 oblong silk scarves, each approximately 68 inches (170cm) long and 22 inches (55cm) wide

2 rings approximately ³/₄ inch (2cm) in diameter

## DIRECTIONS

① Lay one scarf on top of the other, edges matching, on a flat surface.

② With your fingers, gather both layers 22 inches (55cm) from one end.

③ Insert center of gathered section into a ring, and pull scarves through to form 2-inch (5cm) loop.

④ Twist the loop to form a rosette.

⑤ Repeat steps 2–4 to create a rosette at opposite end.

⑥ Separate the scarves between the rosettes to form a stole. Place stole over head, allowing one scarf to drape across the bodice and the other to drape across the back; rosettes should rest on opposite shoulders and ends should cascade freely.

⑦ Arrange the folds as desired.

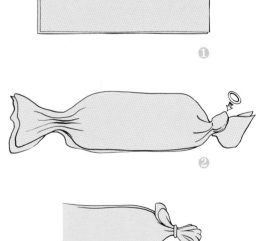

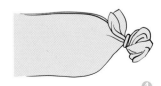

# WOMEN'S CASUAL BLAZER DRAPE AND MEN'S ASCOT

*Threre is no escaping the fact that the blazer is one of the most versatile pieces of clothing in our wardrobes. It is easy to dress up or dress down, and it looks as great with a slim skirt and silk shirt as it does with stone-washed jeans and a vest. In this ensemble, the classic combination of starched white shirt and blazer is refined and made more feminine by the addition of a rolled scarf draped casually around the neck. The ends of the scarf can also be slipped behind the edges of the lapel for a narrower slash of color. The same rolled scarf could also be worn under the collar of a shirtwaist dress or the full ruffled collar of a poet's blouse.*

*Dressing up the man's camel blazer is an ascot, shown here in an open-neck shirt with button-down collar. Though usually associated with the smoking jacket or satin-lapelled robe, the ascot has moved into casual daytime wear, and is especially perfect for cooler spring evenings. Try wearing the ascot with a mid-weight V-neck sweater; it looks fabulous.*

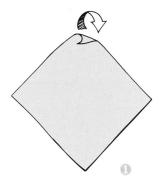

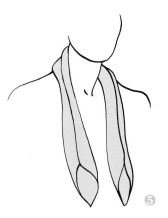

## MATERIALS FOR CASUAL BLAZER DRAPE

1 scarf approximately 30 inches (75cm) square

## DIRECTIONS

① Lay scarf on a flat surface with points at top and bottom.

② Beginning at the top point, roll the scarf down to the horizontal center.

③ Roll the bottom up to the horizontal center.

④ Center the scarf, rolls facing outward, at the back of the neck.

⑤ Bring the ends to the front and drape gently along the inner edge of blazer lapel.

# MATERIALS FOR MEN'S ASCOT

1 oblong scarf approximately 50 inches (125cm) long and 11 inches (27.5cm) wide

## DIRECTIONS

❶ Fold scarf in half lengthwise.

❷ Center scarf at back of neck with fold at top; bring ends to front.

❸ Cross right end over left end (a); bring right end up behind left end toward chin (b), then down over left end to form knot.

❹ Tighten knot until comfortable, then adjust folds of scarf to full width.

❺ Tuck ends into shirt.

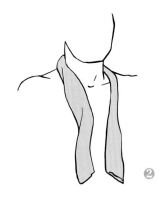

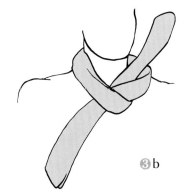

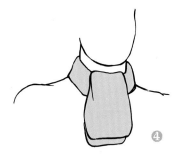

# MEN'S MUFFLER AND WOMEN'S PEASANT-STYLE CAPE

*Two classics—an oversized shawl in navy and cream and a hand-woven oblong scarf in camel and light blue—are teamed up in this stylish ensemble. Although worn here with traditional blazers, both wraps will complement a wide range of fashion styles. Adding wraps in different patterns and colors will give virtually any piece of apparel greater versatility. The cape is especially appealing when worn as a shawl over a winter coat or raincoat.*

*You needn't limit wearing large square scarves to the shoulder area. They can be wrapped in any number of pleasing ways according to your personal taste. Try wrapping a large square scarf folded into a triangle around a long print skirt to form a peasant-style sash. Or wrap an oversized cotton shawl into a sarong for summer wear, and pair it with an easygoing men's broadcloth shirt tied at the midriff.*

## MATERIALS FOR MEN'S MUFFLER

1 oblong wool scarf approximately 48 inches (120cm) long and 10 inches (25cm) wide

## DIRECTIONS

① Center scarf at front of neck.

② Bring ends around to back of neck and cross.

③ Bring ends to front of neck, allowing them to drape gently down front of lapels.

④ Adjust scarf for desired looseness and comfort.

61

## MATERIALS FOR WOMEN'S PEASANT-STYLE CAPE

1 scarf approximately 48 inches (120cm) square

## DIRECTIONS

① Lay scarf on a flat surface with points at top and bottom.

② Fold top point down 4 inches (10cm) past center.

③ Arrange scarf on shoulders so that both points show and bottom point falls at middle of back. Bring ends to front.

④ Bring right end across front of neck and drape over left shoulder.

⑤ Bring left end across front slightly below neck and drape over right shoulder.

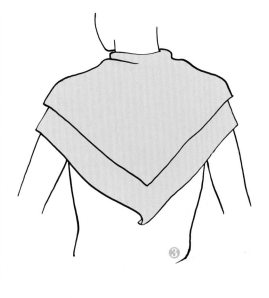

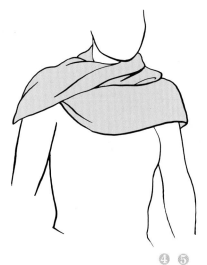

# MEN'S POCKET SCARF I

*The strong palette of this silk pocket square lends elegance to the traditional camel blazer, adding flourish to an otherwise smooth, polished look. For a less dramatic accent, push the folded scarf deeper into the pocket. For a bolder look, pull the corners of the scarf to create longer ends of colorful accent, allowing the ends to cascade unevenly above and below the edge of the pocket.*

## MATERIALS

1 scarf approximately 20 inches (50cm) square

## DIRECTIONS

① Lay scarf on a flat surface.

② Pinch scarf at the center and lift.

③ Draw scarf through a circle formed by thumb and forefinger to create even gathers.

④ Still holding scarf at top, fold lower section up 2 inches (5cm).

⑤ Insert scarf, folded edge first, into jacket breast pocket, allowing ends to cascade over the pocket edge.

# MEN'S POCKET SCARF II

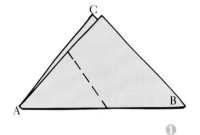

*No collection would be complete without the traditional folded pocket scarf shown in the photograph. Easy to fold and always refined and sophisticated in appearance, the pocket scarf is an indispensable accent to the well-dressed man. Whether a paisley, overall print, stripe, or geometric scarf is chosen, this style of fold looks equally dignified and polished. Coordinate the color of the jacket with the color of the scarf (and the neck tie) to create an appealing match. For a more dramatic fashion statement, choose a scarf that is a complement of the color of the jacket (for example, pair a melon pocket square with a lavender blazer, or match a navy blazer with a lemon yellow scarf). The contrast will draw great attention.*

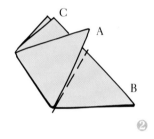

## MATERIALS

1 pocket scarf

## DIRECTIONS

1 Fold scarf in half diagonally to form a triangle. Lay it on a flat surface with fold at bottom.

2 Put your right thumb at the midpoint of the fold. Fold left side up, against your thumb, so that point A crosses edge BC.

3 Repeat step 2 to fold point B.

4 Fold the side edges in.

5 Holding the top securely, fold lower section 1 inch (2.5cm) to back.

6 Insert folded scarf into jacket breast pocket, making sure points show above pocket edge.

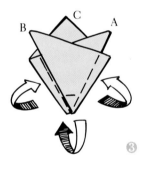

# WOMEN'S COLLAR AND MEN'S OPERA SCARF

*This sumptuous drape of silk printed in rich turquoise and gold is the perfect counterpoint for a tailored coatdress in white. Formed simply by folding a large square into a triangle and allowing the luxurious gathers of fabric to drape in a soft swag across the back, this elegant style takes you from day wear to evening wear in an instant.*

*Just as quickly, the traditional opera-length scarf changes the mood of a classic man's blazer to one of refined and stylish elegance. Small caramel-colored dots are sprinkled liberally across a field of obsidian-black wool crepe on this scarf. For a bolder look, choose a paisley or striped scarf that picks up the color of the blazer in order to pull the pieces together; add a coordinating tie to further enhance the look.*

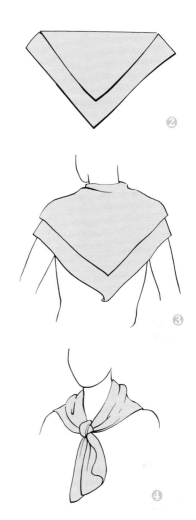

## MATERIALS FOR WOMEN'S COLLAR

1 print scarf with gold metallic detailing, approximately 33 inches (82.5cm) square

## DIRECTIONS

① Lay scarf on a flat surface with points at top and bottom.

② Fold top point down 2 inches (5cm) past center.

③ Arrange scarf on shoulders so that bottom point falls at middle of back.

④ Bring ends to front and tie in a loose double knot at center of neck.

⑤ Slide knot to right shoulder, allowing scarf to slip down back in soft, U-shaped folds.

## MATERIALS FOR MEN'S OPERA SCARF

1 oblong wool crepe scarf approximately 48 inches (120cm) long and 10 inches (25cm) wide

## DIRECTIONS

① Center scarf at back of neck.

② Bring ends to front, allowing them to drape gently over front of lapels.

# SCARF CARE

| FIBER | DRY-CLEAN | WASH | | | | DRYING TEMP. | IRON SETTING | NOTES |
|---|---|---|---|---|---|---|---|---|
| | | HAND | MACHINE | WATER TEMP. | MILD DETERGENT | | | |
| Cotton | Yes | Yes | Yes | Hot | Yes | Medium | High (Iron when damp.) | Fabric softener recommended. Do not overdry. |
| Linen | Yes* | Yes | Yes | Warm | Yes | Low | High (Iron when very damp.) | Wash if label says "pre-shrunk." |
| Silk | Yes* | Yes | No | Lukewarm | Yes | Low | Low (Iron on wrong side.) | Wash if label says "washable." Avoid prolonged exposure to sunlight. |
| Wool | Yes* | Yes | No | Cool | No | — | Medium (Iron with damp press cloth.) | Do not machine-dry. |
| Synthetics | Yes | Yes | Yes | Lukewarm | Yes | Medium | Low–Medium | Follow cleaning instructions on label. |

*Preferred cleaning method

# INDEX